GLUE

Making Your Family Stick

// Joel Southerland

CONTENTS

FOREWORD

THE EMBRAER LEGACY 600 is one of the most beautiful and most popular private jets on the market. I hear they are also fun to fly. To learn to fly one you need two things. First, you need the flight manual created by the manufacturer. Second, you need a competent flight instructor with lots of experience.

It's no different when you want to fly your *marriage* well. If you're looking for a solid takeoff, insightful navigation, and a safe landing without falling out of the sky, you've got the right book in your hands.

There's no more important relationship in your life outside of Jesus than your marriage. It's the first relationship God instituted and the only one that has the special status of two-becoming-one.

This book is based on God's flight manual for marriage: the Bible. Joel Southerland sees the Word of God as the "final authority for faith and practice"—especially when it comes to marriage.

I can tell you this book is also the result of sifting though God's Word on marriage through Joel's competent experience in the marriage cockpit with his sweet bride, Sherry.

Just as you don't get financial advice from a broke financial advisor, you don't go to a relationship guru that's been divorced a few times (unless you're trying to learn what not to do).

Joel and Sherry have an exemplary marriage. I cannot think of anyone else I know that has had a more consistently successful marriage. Yes, they've had their struggles like any other marriage. But they have learned to maximize one another's strengths, overcome one another's weaknesses, bridge the valleys, rebound from the losses, and even more than that, teach others to do the same.

But then there's an added perspective not held by many who train on marriage. Joel is a pastor. A pastor gets to peek behind the curtain on so many lives. You know that couple that everybody thought was doing great and then their divorce surprised everyone? The pastor saw that coming. You know the new marriage of the couple who had dated five years that everybody knew was going to be one of the best for years to come, but then divorced after year one? The pastor saw that coming. Joel the biblicist can tell you what the Bible teaches about marriage. Joel the married guy can tell you from his experience what he's learned to do and not do in a marriage to a particular person that shares some similarities with others. But Joel the pastor can tell you as someone who's "seen it all."

So, congratulations, you're actually reading a book that you don't have to take with a grain of salt. You can drink deeply of these principles for your marriage and immediately put them into practice. By doing so, you'll be flying higher, further, and longer in your marriage than you ever thought you could. And even better, you'll one day enjoy the safe landing that fewer and fewer marriages get to experience.

Scott N. Smith
Online Training Strategist, Georgia Baptist Mission Board
President, SNS Ministries Inc.

CHAPTER ONE

// Let's Talk

LEO TOLSOY, THE famous Russian novelist, wrote these words to begin his massive tome, *Anna Karenina*: "All Happy families are alike; each unhappy family is unhappy in its own way."

Indeed.

Sadly, as a pastor who does his fair share of counseling, it has been my observation that there are far too many unhappy families in America today. So many families are becoming *unglued*.

I have a burden to find ways to help. I want to be practical, but never at the expense of Biblical truth. I want to be doctrinally sound, but never at the expense of practical application. Let's explore some ways to keep families from becoming unglued. We must begin with our marriages, and I have isolated several ways to make marriage *stick*.

But first, have you ever considered the impact of a happy marriage on how long you will live? There is actually research suggesting that those of us in happy marriages have a 20% less chance of dying too early. The *Journal of Health Psychology* conducted a survey and noticed a correlation between an unhappy marriage and actually wanting to die.

The bottom line is that a happy marriage is good for your health. There is even evidence that a happy marriage can lead to a healthier heart and trimmer waist line! Professor Mark Weisman was one of the authors of the study and he concluded that marriage provides us with meaningful roles, a strong identity, a sense of purpose, and pervasive feelings of security. All of these are keys to good mental health and well-being—and therefore great for us *physically*.

So there you have it, if you are in a happy marriage you can be like Mr. Spock—*live long and prosper!* But it's not science fiction—it's science. Better yet, it's *creation* science. Weisman says, "A high quality marriage can serve as a buffer against chronic or acute stressors in life."

The other side of the coin is that unhappy marriages link us to poor physical health—even putting us at greater risk for things like high blood pressure and heart disease. This is because marital stress leads to emotional distress and physical pain.

Along with "quality of life" issues, there is also the matter of how this impacts our Christian witness. Unhappy marriages in the church are certainly no great advertisement for the power of the gospel before a lost and dying world.

I think most of us would agree that society in general would be better off with more happy marriages and families. But how can we, as the church, criticize the larger culture, when there are troubles on our own doorstep?

I want to share several ways to make a marriage stick—stick like *glue*.

Everything will be backed with Scripture and include very practical advice. Let's start with *communication*. There's no doubt about it—happy couples talk more.

Much more.

Wise old King Solomon wrote three books found in the Old Testament. One was about wisdom, another was about futility, and then there is one he wrote about love. It's called the Song of Solomon. It's a dialogue between a bride and groom—a husband and wife. Many see it as a beautiful allegory about Christ and the church, or God and Israel, which is, of course a valid interpretation. But it was primarily an intimate expression of genuine marital love.

There's a lot we can learn about marriage from the Song of Solomon, but one verse seems to capture the spirit of the book: *"O my dove, in the clefts of the rock, in the secret places of the cliff, let me see your face. Let me hear your voice for your voice is sweet and your face is lovely."*[1]

He had a pet name for his bride. It's clear that their relationship thrived on communication. They liked to talk to each other. It's like that in every happy marriage. Husbands and wives talk to each other, spend time alone together, and each spouse enjoys the continual process of getting to know the other one better.

Studies find that happy couples talk an average of five hours a day. You have to talk to each other, you have to communicate, you have to share, and you have to be willing to open up. A happy marriage requires a major amount of communication.

Younger couples, particularly—with work challenges and dealing with growing children—find it hard to make time to just talk. But you have got to figure it out. You've got to figure out how to call one another during the day, or even send a text. It's never been easier to communicate than it is right now. Take advantage of technology and use it for good. Of course, you also must figure out how to sit down and talk *face-to-face*.

I travel a lot during the week. It seems like I'm always about to get on a plane to go somewhere. So, I have to make a very special effort. I'll get to my hotel du jour and the first thing I do is to open my *iPad* and *FaceTime* my wife for a while, just reliving every part of the day.

When my wife Sherry and I first started dating, she was 15 almost 16, I was 16 almost 17. We met at what we began to call the "Love Shack," *Shop Rite* grocery store in Chatsworth. There were no cell phones, there was no Internet, so no *Facebook*. Here's what we had: a landline telephone and a mailman.

Now, before some of the younger readers reach for their phones to *Google* (something else we didn't have) "landline," let me explain. It was a communication device usually tethered to a nearby wall by a cord. The longer the cord, the cooler you were, because you could walk around while on your phone. Sherry had a cord on her kitchen phone that was about 100 feet long.

She was very cool.

Her parents were strict, so we could only date once a week. The only way I could communicate with her was at church. So I started going to church all the time. I showed up Sunday morning, Sunday night, Wednesday night, WMU, visitation, I helped to clean the church—you name it. I was there all the time. I'd write letters and go by and put them in her mailbox, and I'd take a letter from her with me.

We started calling each other every day. Back then, there was something called "long distance." I lived in Gordon County. She lived in Murray County. This meant that all of our calls were "long distance," which meant there were extra charges for each minute on the line. One month, I ran up a phone bill of more than $200. My parents weren't impressed, and my dad forbade me from calling her ever again from the home phone.

So, I started using a payphone.

A payphone was basically a phone (with a cord) on a stand in the middle of rough place somewhere. And a payphone was open to the elements. It also had enough germs on it to send the CDC into meltdown. No one cleaned a payphone. That was the rain's job.

I risked my life to call Sherry using a payphone every day.

I attended Dalton College and one day they canceled our night classes because of snow and ice. It took me nine tries to get up a hill to a little shopping center. It was high tech—they had four pay phones right there like in a little cluster. I was the only diehard out there in the snow on the phone with my pocket full of quarters.

Sherry asked, "What are you doing?"

"Well, there are three inches of snow on the ground and it's 29 degrees," I replied, peeling the cold phone from my face.

She went into the utility room and sat on the washing machine to talk. I stood there in the freezing cold, plugging quarter after quarter into the cash-hungry telephone. Why? Because I wanted to communicate. But what happens when you get married? Communication slows down and sometimes stops.

You have to keep talking.

Let me share some "don'ts" about communication. First, don't assume communication has actually been taking place. You may have used all of your words today, but your spouse may not have and you still need to talk.

Second, don't assume your spouse intuitively knows what you mean. There are many unnecessary arguments because one assumes the other one understood.

Third, never raise your voice. Arguing is not communicating. If you find yourself shouting, you are not communicating.

Fourth, don't withdraw. Sometimes a spouse will shut down and turn off communication. This is the worst thing in the world for a marriage.

Finally, don't talk to anyone else more than you talk to your spouse. If these words ever come out of your mouth,

"Boy, I can talk to you so much better than I can my wife or my husband," you should get right with God immediately, and start talking to your spouse.

Now, let me share some things you should "do." Number one, ask open-ended questions. Don't just ask "how was your day?" Say it like this: "Tell me about your day." It gives your spouse something to expand on.

Number two, save some things for face-to-face communication. There are times something exciting happens during the day and I'll text it to myself to remind myself to talk about it that evening with my wife when we go out to eat or sit down in the recliners. I save some great stuff for when we are together.

Number three, actually care about what the other person cares about. You need to care about what your spouse cares about.

Number four, put the digital devices down when you are together. You've seen the couple at the restaurant, right? They haven't seen each other all day. It's six o'clock. They're eating together. And what are they both doing? And they haven't said a word to each other because they're doing this. When you have your spouse face to face, set your phone down.

Happy couples talk more.

Notes

[1] Song of Solomon 2:14

CHAPTER TWO

// Cheerleading & Conflict

ANOTHER THING WE know about happy couples is that they tend to encourage more. One of my favorite verses in the Bible says, *"Let no corrupt word proceed out of your mouth but what is good for necessary edification that it may impart grace to the hearers."*[A] When the text says "necessary edification," it literally means "good for encouragement."

Happy couples cheer each other on, they encourage one another, build the other one up. Marriage should be full of encouragement. The Bible bears that out. We are all supposed to be encouragers. And that doesn't mean just people at church or at work. It should start at home. One study found that when happy couples encourage each other, they give *compliments*. They also show appreciation for things big and small. They don't take anything for granted. They do nice things for each other. And they like to relive fun memories.

These are encouraging things.

Happy spouses are cheerleaders for each other—big time. Sherry is my biggest cheerleader. It's one of the reasons our marriage is so great today. When I preach a sermon, she tells me it's the best sermon she's ever heard. Every week. I know it's not, but I sure don't mind the sentiment. She's even taught our daughters to do it. Mikayla will call me and she'll say, "Dad, that was the best." I just feel like I'm getting better and better and better at this. Savana will do the same thing. One time, when we were living in Atlanta, I walked in the front door and all three of my girls were at the landing and they started clapping for me. I don't even know what I did. But I must be awesome at something.

I am blessed to be surrounded by encouragers.

I went in our kitchen to fix a cup of coffee in the kitchen early one Saturday morning—it happened to be my birthday. There were *Post-it* notes all around, messages from my wife. Words of encouragement. Emotional encouragement. Spiritual encouragement. She called me her favorite preacher. She even told me I had sexy legs.

That one was on the refrigerator.

Happy spouses encourage each other all the time. Let me give you one "don't" and one "do." Don't tear down and discourage. If you're always pointing out faults, you will never have a happy marriage. I know some of you are thinking, "but he's a mess." Yet, you married that mess. You ask, "how am I going to fix him?" You should have done that before you walked down the aisle. You say, "I thought things would get better when we got married." Here's what you're going to have to do, you're going to have to learn to overlook some things, live with some things, and have some patience with some things. You can help your spouse become a better person but it's going to take some time. You can't nag it out of him or her. Constant negativity is a sure pathway to a miserable marriage. Always be a cheerleader. Constantly compliment—this needs to be the theme of your home life.

There's another thing about happy marriages—happy couples know how to fight *better*. My wife quotes Proverbs 15:1 all the time, *"A soft answer turns away wrath but a harsh word stirs up anger."* You've got to learn how to give a soft answer and fight better. I read a study that said, the more you fight early on in marriage and *work through it*, the happier and stronger your marriage will be later on.

You are going to argue, and those first few years might actually be pretty rough. Things change after you get married. You thought you were getting *The Notebook* and you got *Rambo*. You want him to follow you through a lily field at night, he wants a bag of *Doritos* and a ball game, and he's not going to change.

So, you fight.

The first time you saw her without makeup was the morning after and you were like, oh my goodness, where's my wife? The first few years can be rough. But if you're arguing five—or twenty-five—years into the marriage the same way you did in year one, something is wrong. You've got to learn to fight better and healthier. And that means learning to give a soft answer. Unhappy spouses criticize each other. They show contempt or a lack of respect. They roll their eyes—a lot. They act defensively. They tune out. Tuning out leads to checking out because they cease to care. And they tend to default to name calling.

That's a long way from Solomon's *"Oh my dove."*

Now, when happy couples find themselves in an argument, they show and use *humor*. It's hard to do sometimes, but if you step back and make fun of yourself, it can work. Humor should never be at your spouse's expense. But if you make fun of yourself, you can neutralize a fight.

Happy couples also express affection. It is hard to fight with somebody when they're hugging you.

They also know how to *give in*. Have you ever been in the middle of an argument and you think, "I don't even really care about what we're fighting about"? But then, you dig in and keep fighting. You know why? Because you've already drawn a line in the sand and you're going to look like an idiot if you back down. You want to save face.

Go ahead and look like an idiot. Say, "You know what, I'm stupid. I don't even care about this. I am a moron. Yeah, I agree with you, honey, you're right." When you find yourself in the middle of an argument that you don't care about, back out. When you find yourself in the middle of an argument that you do care about, sometimes choose to give in. If the fate of humanity is not at stake, let it go. You can be right or in love, your choice.

It's not always possible to be both.

Brigham Young University did a study about fighting via text. Here's what they discovered, that couples who argue over text, apologize over text, and/or attempt to make decisions over text are *less* happy in their relationships than couples who fight and argue face to face.

Happy couples keep kids in the right place. Look at Genesis 2:24. *"Therefore shall a man leave his father and mother and shall be joined to his wife. And they shall become one flesh."* You and your spouse are one flesh until the day you die. Husband plus wife equals one. Husband plus wife plus kid equals how many? Two. When kids come, life can get crazy. They take up a lot of couple time, and very unintentionally, they can drive a wedge between mom and dad. So here's what happens. All of a sudden, all of this energy that you were pouring into your spouse, you now have to pour into a child. But if you're not careful, you'll keep the children's tank full and you spouse's tank will be empty.

When your children grow up and move out, you're going to be strangers in the same house because you've put all of your energy into your kids. God never meant for your kids to take the place or the energy of your spouse. Your kids are going to leave you one day, or they're going to move to the basement, one or the other, they're getting out of the main part of the house. Like I used to ask Mikayla, my youngest daughter, when she was five years old, "Who are you going to marry when you grow up?" And she'd say, "Daddy." I'd say, "That's right, sign right here, right here on the dotted line." She married Josh. My girls, they're in love with their husbands.

They left me.

Your children *are* going to leave you one day. And there is an epidemic of divorce for people in their 50s, when they become empty nesters. How do you prevent that? First, let your children know that your spouse is actually number one. My girls will tell you that Sherry loves me most and I love her the same way. We told them that for years. We let our kids know our spouse was number one.

Another key is that we don't keep *secrets*. My girls have never come to me and said, "Dad, I want to tell you something, but don't tell mom." But a few times, they went to Sherry and said, "Mom, I need to tell you something but don't tell dad." And Sherry always said, "I'm telling dad. Just so you know, dad and I keep no secrets." Now, she may choose the right time to tell me, which is normally in a public place at a restaurant right after dessert, but she always told me. She always told the girls she was going to tell me.

Do not keep secrets—they drive a wedge.

Now, my next thought may be hard for some of you to digest because you have kids at home. But stay with me. Do things *without* your kids. You need date nights. If you want a great marriage, find someone to watch the children, pay them whatever it takes, and go out—just the two of you. We never had a lot of grand-parental support with our kids when they got older so we'd find somebody watch our kids and we'd go on a date night, regularly. It's essential.

One of the greatest things we ever did was when Mikayla was in middle school, and Savana was in early high school. We had a friend who kept our kids and Sherry and I went to Florida all by ourselves. We rented a condo on a golf course and guess what we did all week? We went to Disney World *without* our kids. It was the best thing ever. Couples pushing baby strollers and dragging four-year-old's behind them. And we were there by ourselves.

It was awesome.

Never let them see you fight. You're going to fight, but don't do it in front of the children. When you fight in front of your kids, you force them to emotionally take sides, to the detriment of your marriage and family. It may make you feel good in the moment, but it's hurting your marriage. Don't ever fight in front of your kids. Instead, show affection in front of them. That's right, kiss in front of your kids. Good old lip smacking kisses. Not pecks on the cheek. Go in hard.

We went to *Community Pie & Pizza* in downtown Chattanooga a while back for my birthday. Mikayla and Josh just had a brief moment to get away from the hospital to meet us there. I dropped my wife off and parked. When I came back, I was the last one to slide into the booth. I slid in next to Sherry, I put my arms around her waist and pulled her in tight and planted a big one on her. We lost ourselves for just a moment until Mikayla and Josh told us to knock it off. We've done that all through our marriage.

I don't care what you think.

Study after study shows the number one thing you can do to raise healthy children is to have a healthy marriage. And we want our kids to know we are in love with one another. So kiss in front of them.

In fact, do that right now.

Notes

[1] Ephesians 4:29

CHAPTER THREE

// Money & Media

HAPPY COUPLES ALSO figure out how to deal with finances. Don't love money, be satisfied with what you have, for God said, *"I'll never leave you, never fail you and I've never abandon you."*[1] You've got to figure money out. According to Dave Ramsey, money is a leading cause of divorce. It's the second leading cause of divorce behind infidelity. And studies show that if you have a high level of debt and lack of communication, you're going to be filled with stress. One study said that if you argue with your spouse once a week about finances, you are 30% more likely to get divorced.

Another study measured young couples at the beginning of a three-year period. There were some couples that had zero dollars in assets. They put them in two categories, zero dollars in assets, or at least $10,000 in assets.

Now, that's not an enormous amount, but for a young couple, it's a good start. The couples who had zero dollars in assets were 70% more likely to get divorced in the three-year period than the couple that had $10,000 in assets. This is all to say money can cause difficult problems in the marriage.

How do we work through money problems? There are only a few certain things you can do. Number one, make more money. Maybe get a little more ambitious, get some more education, whatever you have got to do, you may need to make more. Somebody may need to go to work. You may need an *extra* job, but make more. If you can't make more then you must spend less. You've got to live below your means. Just two ways—it's that simple. And that hard. You must also save some. Could you come up with $2,000 in one week? The majority of Americans would find that very difficult. You need savings.

Happy couples also tend to hang out with the right people. It's a great Proverb, *"He who walks with wise men will be wise, but a companion of fools will be destroyed."*[2] It's true personally, and it's true in your marriage. According to Brown University, if you hang out with a couple that is divorced, you are 75% more likely to get divorced yourself. That's not a religious study. It's a secular study. That means you need to hang out with people who are on solid ground. I'm not telling that you shouldn't help your friends. I'm saying you need to choose your friends carefully, especially your group of friends. You will become like the group of people with whom you hang out. You will grow to resemble them.

So choose your friends carefully.

Not only that. We should have a lot of friends in common. In 2013, *Facebook* analyzed 1.3 million users. Here's what they discovered. People who identified as married, the ones who had crossover friendships, were *less likely* to break up than those who had separate networks. As a matter of fact, *Facebook* discovered that if you had separate networks, got married and brought them together, you were *least* likely to get divorced. So, have the same good group of friends, and be careful that you hang out with the right people.

Speaking of *Facebook* and friends, be very careful with social media and your online presence. I am weary of hearing about breakups and divorces that happen because of *Facebook, Snapchat, Twitter,* and *Instagram*. You have absolutely no business starting a relationship online. There should be no privacy between spouses when it comes to social media. Share passwords. If you send me a private message, my wife can read it. I have a browser on her phone I use to sign into my *Facebook account*, she can look at it anytime she wants to. On *Instagram*, we have double accounts.

Consider this, 81% of the *American Academy of Matrimonial Lawyers* have usually encountered evidence taken from *Facebook* or a social media site. *Facebook* is really helping divorce lawyers nowadays. So be careful who you're hanging out with—even digitally.

Happy couples blend *faith* and *family*. *"Husbands, love your wives just as Christ also loved the church and gave himself for her."* Here's what we're told; that the Christ-church relationship is a depiction of the husband-wife relationship.[3] This tells us that family and faith are to be blended as something very natural.

Spouses who attend church together often (the key word) are 2.4 times less likely to divorce than spouses who are not frequent churchgoers. If you come to church often, you almost eradicate your chances of divorce. Not only that, fathers who attend church frequently are more invested in family life and their wives reported feeling more loved and more satisfied in their marriage.

Let me give you three priorities. Number one— church attendance. I've heard so many families over the years say that church attendance gets in the way of family time. But there is nothing you can do on Sunday that's going to keep your marriage together more than going to church together. You say, "Well, we like to go to the lake in the summertime." There's not one shred of research that says going to the lake together will keep your marriage together. But there's compounding research and evidence that says if you go to church together, then your marriage is more likely to make it. So make church a priority. Go to the lake on Saturday, come back on Saturday night, go to church on Sunday, and go back to the lake after church.

It's worth it to make church a priority.

Number two, find places to *serve*. When we put our faith into action and learn how to meet the needs of others, we are following the example of Jesus. The strongest families in any church are those where spouses serve in ministry. And their children, as they grow up, learn this as a basic value.

Number three, have a *devotional* life. Husbands and wives walk together serving the Lord together. You have a quiet time, she ought to have a quiet time, where you're spending time in the Bible and prayer. You're going to find it hard to be wrong with your spouse and right with God. As a matter of fact, you will find it impossible.

There it is. If you want to make your marriage stick, if you want to make it happy, talk more, encourage more, and fight better. Keep kids in the right place, figure out your finances, hang out with the right people, and blend faith and family.

Notes

[1] Hebrews 12:5
[2] Proverbs 13:20
[3] Ephesians 5:25

CHAPTER FOUR

// Pro Parenting

SOMETIMES WE GET the feeling that our families are falling apart. We worry about our marriages. We doubt our parenting skills. We wish we communicated better with those we love. We fight over finances. In today's culture, it is clear that on many levels the family is, in fact, becoming unglued. No matter what our struggle, Scripture can point us to the love and power of God—to glue it all back together.

This is especially true when it comes to the hard work of parenting. There are clear spiritual principles to help parent like a pro.

When our first child, Savana, was born I was twenty-two-years old. She was born three-and-a-half-weeks before her due date. Thankfully, she was healthy and only had to stay in the hospital for one extra day. I remember so vividly the day we were to bring her home. I can still see my beautiful wife, Sherry, sitting on the bed and dressing Savana in the tiny dress that she had chosen for her homecoming. I looked at her and said, "So what's the deal? Are they just going to let us walk out of here with this baby?"

She looked at me and said, "Yeah baby. That's what we do. We walk out." I was hoping they would at least show us an instructional video. I had no idea how to be a parent. I had never changed a diaper. I had no idea what I was going to do. I was terrified that I was somehow going to drill through the soft spot on her head and kill her. Shouldn't I have to get some sort of license before they just let me walk out of the hospital with her?

But that's not how it works.

Like other first time parents, we left the hospital with our newborn daughter and we figured it out one day at a time. The first blow out diaper. The first bath time. The joy of the first time she slept through the night. We learned how to parent by parenting. In the beginning it was so hard. But as we gained experience and confidence, it was less scary. It was more manageable.

Our children are now 25 and 29. We made it through those difficult years. Now we are empty nesters. We were not perfect parents. We made many mistakes over the years, and yet, despite our failings, our children turned out to be awesome human beings. Parenting is hard. But I believe in this day and age we often make it much harder than it has to be.

We complicate it.

Bear in mind that I am from the generation when our parents would send us outside in the summertime with a jug of iced *Kool-Aid* and lock the door when we left. We stayed outside twelve hours a day. Mom brought our food outside and told us not to come into the house. You may ask, "Didn't she worry about you?" Yes—that I would try to come back in the house!

We went from that generation to a generation obsessed with our children. And, as with all obsessions, we often go overboard. This is not meant to be offensive. Of course our children's safety is important. But I believe it is possible to *over-parent*. We are helicopter parents. We worry too much. We try too hard.

Consider the recent news about the celebrity parents who were arrested for making fake donations and falsifying records in an attempt to get their children into Georgetown, Yale, Stanford, and USC. More than 50 people have been charged and $25 million dollars was spent in this enormous scheme by well-to-do parents to provide for their children something that was not rightfully theirs. The FBI sting that uncovered this crime was called *Operation Varsity Blues*. The guilty people who were arrested suggested that they were just trying to be good parents.

This begs the question: What makes a good parent? And, even more important, how do we become good and *Godly* parents? Before we can completely dive into this, we first need to understand seven important principles about how parenting works.

First, children are naturally *impressionable*. It is their tendency to pick up and then magnify the bad habits of those around them—especially their parents. What parents do in moderation, children seem to do in excess. So we have to take care what impression and values we are imparting to our children.

Second, children are *resilient*. They bounce back faster than we do. This does not excuse us from harming them. Poor parenting can cause great harm in our children.

Third, parents never get it *right* 100% of the time. We do not do everything right. We can read all the books. We can watch *YouTube* videos. We can get advice from smart people. But we are going to make mistakes.

Fourth, we will get *some things* right. If we love our kids, we are getting it right. There will be good days and bad days, good moments and bad moments. But we will get it right much of the time.

Fifth, sometimes things are out of a parent's hands. It is not all up to the parent. God has a hand in it. Sometimes children who are raised by horrible parents grow up to be healthy, kind, and successful adults. Some children who are raised by parents who are far from God grow up to be faithful followers of Jesus Christ. God is ultimately in control. All we can do as parents is pray that God takes our parenting, our mistakes, our successes, and uses all of it to make our children into who He created them to be. The results of our parenting are largely out of our hands. The results are often up to the child.

Teenagers are a great reminder of this. As parents we do what we think is right, but ultimately the result is up to them. Environment plays a factor. Friends play a factor. Their choices play a factor. Their attitudes play a factor. Their physical and mental health play a factor.

Sixth, we cannot judge the movie by a snapshot. During the active years we raise our children we will have ups and downs. Wins and losses. Triumphs and failures. When things are going well we want to take the credit. We want to write a parenting book (Don't write the book!). When things are going poorly we want to give them up for adoption. Don't give up. Don't look at the snapshot of today's situation. Watch the whole movie. See the big picture.

Finally, parenting is a *process*, not an event. It is a marathon, not a sprint. We always strive to do better. We try not to make the same mistakes over and over. And we pray often.

Understanding these principles is crucial to parenting like a pro.

I see at least five keys to *Parenting like a Pro*.

Number one, to be a healthy parent, be a healthy *person*. Have your life together. Matthew 7:3–5 says, *"Why do you look at the speck in your brother's eye but do not consider the plank in your own eye? Or how can you say to your brother, 'Let me remove the speck from your eye,' and look, a plank is in your own eye? Hypocrite! First remove the plank from your own eye, and then you will see clearly to remove the speck from your brother's eye."*

This may seem to be a peculiar passage of Scripture for a lesson on parenting. But it does apply, because the first thing we need to understand about parenting is that our children are a reflection of us as their parents. If we do not have our lives together it will be reflected in our children. We know this is true. When we see certain traits in our children, we can see ourselves in them. They have our good qualities.

They have our bad qualities. They have our quirks. They have our humor. They have similar personalities. Children are a reflection of their parents.

God even allowed children to physically look like their parents. There is a physical resemblance. When a baby is born people are quick to notice who the newborn looks like. But it is not just a physical reflection. Children often are a reflection of their parents in the way they live. We see it with toddlers. They start acting like their parents. They mimic their actions, mannerisms, and words. And this carries on and is magnified as they get older.

Children can see hypocrisy immediately. Their brains are wired that way. For example, if a parent tells a child to eat his vegetables, and the child notices that the parent has left one green bean on his plate, the child will say, "Well, you didn't finish your vegetables. Why do I have to finish mine?" When a parent tells a child that she has to go to bed at 9:00, she may reply, "Why don't you have to go to bed?" They spot inconsistency and see it as hypocrisy. They mimic their parents, so we have to be the better person in order to be a better parent.

To be better parents it is important to have good marriages. All research, secular and non-secular, shows that a good marriage is important to a child's wellbeing. If parents are fighting, and there is constant stress in the home, it negatively affects parenting. We learn this from more than 50 medical studies that show a link between parental stress and childhood illness, both physical and mental.

A stressed-out marriage produces a stressed-out child.

A stressful marriage makes for bad parenting. In order to be a better parent we must have a better marriage. Kids are more apt to thrive when father and mother love one another.

To be better parents we need to manage our financial, emotional, and spiritual wellbeing. If we want our children to be successful in life and have financial, emotional, and spiritual health, then we have to show the way by how *we* live. We have to model a healthy relationship with our finances. We have to have healthy and balanced emotions. We have to model a healthy spiritual life by living in relationship with Christ.

Our sin, habits, and language will be mimicked and magnified by our children. What they see us do they will do. What they hear us say, they will say. Our attitudes will become their attitudes. Our fears will become their fears. Our hurts will become their hurts. Our stresses will become their stresses. To be better parents we have to limit the negative influence of our own lives onto our children. To be better parents we must always be growing into better people. We should always be learning. Always improving. Always developing our skills. Always striving to be better.

If you were to walk into our house, you would swear that my wife obsessively uses books to *decorate*. Over the years we have bought hundreds, if not thousands of books. The office is filled with books. Every room is overflowing with books. If you went through the house and looked through the titles and subjects of the books, you would see that the vast majority of those books in our home are on marriage, home, and family. How to be a better wife. How to be a better husband. How to have a happy family. How to be a better parents. How to raise a healthy child. Why do we have so

many of these books? Because we were attempting to grow
and become better people, so that we could be better parents.

CHAPTER FIVE

// Fun, Games, & Boundaries

THE SECOND KEY to parenting like a pro is that we should strive as parents to have a happy home. Colossians 3:21 says, *"Fathers, do not provoke your children, lest they become discouraged."* Proverbs 17:22 says, *"A merry heart does good, like medicine, but a broken spirit dries the bones."*

If our homes are full of stress, anger, anxiety, and yelling, our kids are going to be less happy. We will notice that as they grow, they will decide to spend more and more time away from the home. Instead of inviting their friends over, they will choose to spend time at *their* houses. We should not allow our homes to be filled with so much drama that our children seek to escape. Our homes should be places of calm solace that our children run to when they are stressed. The place where other kids want to be.

But so often this is not the case.

When Sherry and I were raising our kids, we talked about it and decided that our goal was to make our home the most fun, joy-filled, happiest home it could be. We wanted our children to bring their friends to our house. Not because we had the best toys, or the newest gadgets, or a great deal of money, but because we had the best loving atmosphere.

When our kids were growing up, there was a revolving door children came through. There were always extra kids in our home. Our girl's friends loved spending time with Sherry. It was not uncommon for my daughter to ask where her friend had disappeared only to find her sitting in our bedroom speaking with Sherry. My wife was a great listener. She did not offer advice unless she was asked. She encouraged the children, and always tried to show a spirit of joy and peace in the home.

When our girls were younger we would take them and their friends to *Chuck E Cheese*. I have very fond memories of Chuck E Cheese. The pizza was not very good, but the games were fun. When life was stressful we knew we could forget our worries for a little while and just enjoy family time at *Chuck E. Cheese*.

The Bible says, *"Do not provoke."*[1] That word in the greek means "to irritate, make angry, or stir up." The Bible teaches that if we have an irritating home, our children will become discouraged, and we will break their spirit. But, a happy home *encourages* children. A happy home is like a good medicine. You have heard the phrase "laughter is the best medicine." Laughter in a home is a sign of health.

How can we make happy homes? First, as parents we should listen instead of lecturing. Constantly lecturing our children closes them off and drives them away. They will not open up to us if we constantly use it against them and turn it into a lecture. Instead we should learn to ask questions and then simply listen to what they have to say. Value their thoughts and opinions.

Another way to build happiness in the home is by playing together. Studies have shown that playing outside is good for the family. Playing card games and board games can bring families closer. Be intentional about spending time together just having fun and talking and laughing with each other. Play basketball. Play video games together. Tell each other jokes.

To build a happy home we must remember that our burdens are not our children's burdens. They do not need to carry the burden of the household. It is the parent's responsibility to carry the burdens. Our stress should not cause them stress. In a survey of thousands of families, the head of the *Family and Work Institute* asked, "If you were granted one wish about your parents, what would it be?" Most of us would assume that the children would wish for more time or more money. But the number one wish of children was that their parents would be less tired and less stressed.

Studies have also shown that parental stress weakens children's brains. Parental stress depletes a child's immune system, increasing the risk of sickness and disease, including obesity, diabetes, mental illness, and even tooth decay. Our stress cannot be our children's stress. Our burdens cannot be their burden.

I remember when I was a young pastor in my early churches. They were often stressful times. There were some strange and difficult church business meetings. As a pastor I used to dread them. You see, we can never be quite sure what is going to happen in a church business meeting. It has been my experience that people filled with pride or anger can hijack a meeting, which made it difficult to attend to the business that God had laid on my heart. Sometimes it was difficult to maneuver through the personalities and problems to get to the place where I could do what God was calling me to do.

It was stressful.

In those days, every now and then, one of our children would pick up on this stress. They would start to worry. They would ask us in fear if everything was ok. But just because they asked did not mean that this was an opportunity to share my burden with my children. It was not their burden to carry. I wanted to protect them from the ugliness of ministry. So I always answered them by saying everything was fine.

After leaving the business world to go into the pastorate, we fell on difficult financial times. We had almost nothing. There were times when we had to tell our children that we did not have the money for something. But we did not share with them the details of our financial stress. Why not? Because that was our financial burden. The burden was not theirs.

A child is not emotionally equipped to carry our adult burdens. We should never pour out our worries into our children. If there are marital struggles, we should never, ever talk about it with our children. They are not designed to carry this burden. They do not have the emotional strength to handle this burden. They should not have to worry about finances, or marital struggles. As children, they are still in the development stage. They are not in a problem-solving stage of life, at least not at that great magnitude. Our burdens should not and cannot be our children's burdens.

Another important thing for us to do as parents is to *slow down*. I once asked a group of people, "If you could go back and tell yourself one thing about parenting before you left the hospital room with your new child, what would you tell yourself?" The number one answer was to slow down. Our lives are too hectic. Slowing down does not mean ignoring our responsibilities so we can simply hold our babies and play with our kids. We must still be the adults in the family. By slowing down, I mean that we need to organize our lives and prioritize the things that take up precious time in our days and space in our heads, so that we have the time and energy to focus more on the wonderful family God has given us. We are so busy *doing* everything that we do not have time for more important things.

Proverbs chapter 31 gives us an example of a woman who had her life prioritized and organized very well. She did not do less. In fact, she ran multiple businesses. Yet, she knew the value of family through all her endeavors, and because of this her children rose up and called her blessed. Men and women alike can learn from this woman's example. We can prioritize and organize our responsibilities so that we can enjoy our children and provide a good life for and with them.

In fact, we must.

When my children were young and I was pastoring my second church, I would always leave for church early. I enjoyed getting there early so I could have time to mentally, emotionally, and spiritually prepare for the day. I would love to tell you that the only reason I left so early was to spend time in prayer with God. But that was just one of the reasons I liked to arrive at church early. The other reason was that Sunday mornings seemed to be really hectic at my house.

Our house was crazy on Sunday mornings. Two little girls and my wife trying to get ready for church made me crazy. It was always something. One Sunday, Mikayla couldn't find one of her shoes and it made my wife almost late for church. My wife frantically searched for her shoe. She asked Mikayla if she had looked in her closet and Mikayla said she had. Sherry asked her to show her where she had looked. Mikayla pointed to the floor of the closet where she liked to play. No shoe. Sherry then found the lost shoe on the top shelf in the corner of the closet.

During all this time I was praying at the church, worried that they would be late. Sherry was stressed because she couldn't find Mikayla's appropriate shoes for church. Looking back, I wish someone would have told us not to worry about the shoe and just bring her barefoot or in different shoes. But we finally figured out a way to alleviate this stress. We started laying their clothes and shoes out on Saturday night, instead of Sunday morning when we were pressed for time.

It worked so well that we eventually started laying clothes out the night before school, also. From there, we started making changes to other stressful morning routines. For example, we would prepare breakfast and lunch the night before so that in the morning we could be much more efficient.

We discovered that incomplete tasks were robbing us of a happy home. So we worked smarter to make sure we were prepared. There is a phenomenon known as the *Zeigarnik Effect*.[2] Research shows that the human mind hates unfinished tasks. Incomplete tasks incite psychic tension. As long as we leave the task unfinished, our brains are in an uncomfortable position. For example, as long as our bed is not made, or there are dishes in the sink waiting to be washed, there is subconscious stress in our lives.

The remedy to this problem is to clear out time in our lives to reorganize and restructure. We have to prioritize and work smarter and more efficiently to have a happy home. Having a happy home does not mean we are disregarding our responsibilities. But it does take planning and effort. A happy home is one that is organized and all of our tasks are completed in a timely and efficient manner. Only then does our subconscious mind allow us to relax and be happy.

Notes

[1] Ephesians 6:4

[2] https://www.goodtherapy.org/blog/psychpedia/zeigarnik-effect

CHAPTER SIX

// Of Rules & Relationships

NEXT, WE MUST spend *time* with our children. It seems simple. And it really is. The easiest and simplest way to do this is to eat meals together, as a family. Research shows that having even one family dinner per week makes a huge difference in family relationships compared to families who never eat together. It can be in a restaurant or even in the living room. The important thing is to sit down *together*, eat and talk. If meals cannot be eaten together then we need to make it a priority to spend time with our children at other times. We can talk late at night before bed, or plan fun activities to do together. It does not matter what we do, as long as we spend time enjoying one another's company and talking.

When our girls were young and we hadn't been able to spend time with them we would let them skip a day of school. Not all the time. But every so often. That may sound awful to some people. Maybe perfect attendance for our children in school is a priority for some. There is nothing wrong with that. But on the last day of school perfect attendance will get a child a piece of paper, whereas special quality time with parents will reap a lifetime of rewards.

In order to have a happy home we also need to remember that *discipline* is a necessary part of parenting. Discipline is not a dirty word. Proverbs 13:24 says, *"He who spares his rod hates his son, but he who loves him disciplines him promptly."* The word discipline means to restrain, warn, check, correct, rebuke, or instruct. This verse is not necessarily a command to spank our children. Discipline has to be Godly. Discipline must always come from a heart of love. It must be healthy. I am not endorsing or denouncing spanking. I was spanked as a child and it was an effective and healthy form of discipline for me, because it was done from a place of love. I am thankful that my parents loved me enough to teach me what was right or wrong. But I do not believe that we *have* to spank our children. Sometimes it works. Sometimes it doesn't.

Good parenting requires discipline. When we allow our children to live without rules or boundaries we are headed for trouble. Children need to learn that there are boundaries, and when we choose to cross those boundaries or break the rules there are consequences. We have to teach our children this when they are young because it is what the adult world is like. If I do not stop at a red light, I must face the consequence of getting a ticket. I understand that the law to stop at a red light is for my safety and the safety of others around me. If I ignore this rule there may be worse consequences than a simple ticket. Children need the same rules and boundaries so they can grow in understanding of how the world works.

Children naturally believe that the world revolves around them. If they want something they should be able to have it. If they want to do something they should be able to do it. It is up to parents to help shape their understanding and expectation of what they can and cannot do. If we raise children with no boundaries and turn them loose in the world, emotional, mental, and even physical havoc will be the result. The police expect your child to respect rules and boundaries.

Surprisingly, not everyone shares this opinion in our current culture. There is a dangerous book titled, *NurtureShock: New Thinking About Children*. It says that rules and boundaries do not help children, but actually hurt them.

But the Bible teaches otherwise.

Ironically, the parents who are the most consistent in enforcing rules and boundaries are the same parents who are described as the most warm and loving. They are the parents that engaged in conversation with their kids. They have influence in their children's lives. They explain why they have rules and they expect the children to obey them. In other areas of the children's lives they allow the children a certain level of autonomy, allowing them their freedom to make their own choices. Studies even prove that the children of these types of parents lie the least.

So how do we discipline well? First, we have to have clear boundaries in key areas. The two important words are *clear* and *key*. Keep the rules for the big things and be consistent with enforcing these rules. Do not have rules for absolutely everything. Do not have rules just to have rules. Too many rules can backfire.

I must confess that when our first child was young we had many rules. We had a rule for everything. She was a preacher's kid, and I was new in the ministry. We tried to force her to do everything that we wanted her to do. Later in life we actually apologized for being so controlling and strict with her. By the time her little sister came along five years later, we loosened up on the rules a little.

When we have too many rules for our children, the children do not have any autonomy. When we make all of the decisions for our children, they will never learn how to make good choices. They may grow up resenting the rules and when they have the chance, they will do the exact opposite. By the time a child is 18 years old he or she should be capable of making wise decisions. Children cannot do this if they have not been given the space and freedom to practice while under parental supervision. Children have to learn by trial and error, surrounded by the love, support, and understanding of parents.

In order to teach our children how to make good decisions, we have to teach them the why, and not just the what. If we do not have a good why, then we do not have a good rule. There must be a reason for the rule, and the child must know and understand that reason. As parents we must expect obedience from our children. We do not have to bargain for it. We do not scream and yell for it. We must let our children know that we expect it. We should not punish mistakes. Mistakes are an opportunity for our children to grow. Our children learn valuable lessons through their mistakes.

We should always be consistent. We cannot laugh at a behavior today and then punish a child for the same behavior tomorrow. We cannot let them get away with something today and punish them for it tomorrow. Consistency is hard in parenting. But it is absolutely crucial. Without consistency rules will not have importance or meaning to the child.

Sometimes the consequences of bad decisions can be the best teacher for a child. It can be a good thing for our children to face the natural consequences of their bad decisions. We are often too worried about seeing our kids make mistakes, yet they are actually a part of healthy development. When I was around eight years old, we lived in a subdivision on a dirt road and it had a big hill. One night, my daddy told me not to ride my bicycle down the hill.

I chose to do it anyway.

A friend had dared me. I thought I had no choice. I had to take the dare. So I rode down that hill as fast as I could, though my daddy had told me not to do it. As I flew down that hill, I hit a rock. My bike started to wobble and lean to the left. I skidded about 20 yards on the side of my face and body. When I finally skidded to a stop, I rolled over, but I could not get up right away. The whole left side of my face and body was badly scraped. My eye, cheek, arm, and leg were a bloody mess.

But that was nothing compared to the fear I felt when a neighbor went to get my daddy.

They carried me back home and bandaged me up. I wound up missing several days of school because I was so banged up. I was so afraid when the excitement had died down and my daddy entered the room. I just knew that he was going to be angry with me and punish me. When I saw him, I gathered all the courage I could muster and asked, "Daddy, am I going to get a spanking?" He looked at me and said, "No, I think you learned your lesson, didn't you? I didn't want you to ride down the hill because I knew it was dangerous, not because I didn't want you to have fun. I simply didn't want you to get hurt. Did you learn your lesson?"

I sure did.

Sometimes the natural consequence of a bad decision is the best teacher. They can hear truth from us, but sometimes they only believe it when they experience things for themselves. So, we cannot and should not protect them from *every* bad decision. Obviously this does not apply to life threatening situations or very serious matters. But we have to give them room to make their own choices as children—so they can when they are adults.

On the other side of this coin, direct disobedience must have consequences. Defiance must have consequences.

Another important thing to remember in parenting is to teach our children—not just preach at them. Proverbs 4:3–4 says, *"When I was my father's son, tender and the only one in the sight of my mother, he also taught me and said to me, 'Let your heart retain my words. Keep my commands and live.'"* In this passage, we see the writer telling us that his father would basically get him up when he was a young child, take him for a walk, and lovingly show and teach him how to live a blessed, happy, and successful life. He did not just preach to the child when he did something wrong. He took the time and effort to help the child to understand the ways of God and the ways of the world. Sometimes parenting is very hard. Sometimes our human reaction is to yell, barking orders instead of teaching principles. We preach instead of teach.

At the end of the day, what do we want our kids to say about us when they are grown and we are gone? Do we want them to remember the yelling? The rigid rules that made no sense? How they wished we had spent more time with them? Or do we want them to remember how much we loved and cared for them by taking the time to teach them and by making it a priority to spend time with them? Do we want to be remembered for the times we brushed them off because we were too busy? Or do we want them to remember the principles and truth about life that we took the time to teach them? What do we want to teach them? What do we want them to learn from what we say, and more importantly, what we do? Actions always speak louder than words. What attitudes and skills do we want to teach them? Do we want them to treat people kindly and with respect? Do we want them to have basic manners? Do we want them to know how to talk to people?

And most importantly, what do we want them to know about God? Do we want them to walk with God? Do we want them to understand the truth about our sin and God's redemption plan for us? Do we want them to fully grasp how much God loves us and wants a daily relationship with us? As parents we have to teach and model these things for our children. And then we need to reinforce them.

The Bible is our guide. Psalm 110:105 says, *"Your Word is a lamp unto my feet. It is a light unto my path."* As parents we do not follow culture. We do not follow trends. We do not follow society. We do not follow what is popular opinion. We follow God's Word. We follow the Holy Spirit's guidance.

First, everything we teach our children should be rooted in Biblical principles.

Second, if we are teaching our children to follow the Bible, we must be following the Bible ourselves. We cannot tell them to do something if we are not doing it ourselves. Remember, children see hypocrisy.

Third, the church is important. As parents, our attitudes towards the body of Christ, and the teaching and preaching of God's Word goes a long way with our children. We must take caution in speaking harshly against these things in front of our children. We must teach our children to respect the leadership that God has placed in His church. We need to always teach them that our spiritual leaders are to be respected and that we can turn to them in our time of need. If our children hear us complaining about a pastor, or student pastor, they will not respect the authority of those people and will not see them as a help to them. So we need to keep our kids involved in church. It has to be a priority.

Fourth, we should share with our children what we are learning. When we learn something from a sermon or a verse, we should share that insight with our children. When a verse speaks to our hearts, we should let our loved ones share in that truth. When we hear a good sermon, we should tell our family about it. We should discuss these things with our kids. Allow them to be a part of the conversation and ask for their thoughts and opinions.

Finally, we must read the Bible and pray its promises and principles over our children and families. For this to happen we should have a growing and living relationship with Jesus Christ. We should be breathing in the Word of God and applying it to our own lives.

To *parent like a pro* we must, first, have our own lives together. We must have a happy home. We must discipline our children. We must teach instead of preach.

And, we must always use God's Word as our guide.

CHAPTER SEVEN

// Homes of Prayer

SO HOW SHOULD we pray for our families? Let us first consider Ephesians 6:12, which says, *"We are not fighting against flesh and blood enemies, but against evil rulers and authorities of the unseen world, against mighty powers in this dark world, against evil spirits in the heavenly place."*

Sometimes I wonder if prayer really makes a difference? In our current culture, prayer is seen as ineffective. A last resort. A nice sentiment, but what good does it actually do? Do our prayers really mean anything?

First of all, we need to know *why* we should pray.

We should pray because if *we* aren't praying for our own families, then no one is. Years ago when my children were first born I realized that if I am not praying for my children, then probably no one is. It hurt my heart to think of my precious family going through life without being lifted up in prayer. When we are blessed with a family there ought to be a burden in our hearts to pray for them. We should feel a responsibility to pray, because if not us, then who?

Even when we know others are praying for us, it is still our responsibility to pray for those we love. I happen to know that my wife prays, but it is still my responsibility to pray for her and for our family. She knows that I pray, but it is still her responsibility to pray for me and our family. It is a huge blessing that multiple people in our household are intentionally and regularly praying. But I believe that in many homes this is the exception, not the rule. In many homes there is no one praying—for our marriages, for our children, for our parents, and for our grandkids. I pray every day because I could be the only one in a burden of prayer. We should all carry that responsibility.

Second, we pray for our families because we have an enemy determined to destroy us. Scripture is clear that the enemy is on the attack. The spiritual foes of darkness would love to ruin our families. They would love to destroy our happiness, our peace, our chances for success, and our commitment to one another.

It is easy to believe this when things are going bad. But when things are going good in our families we tend to not remember that the enemy is prowling looking for a way to devour us. The enemy wants to ruin and enslave our children to sin. They may be nearly perfect now, but Satan has a plan to destroy them. He wants to put a wedge in our marriages. He wants to destroy our future. He wants our families to be filled with arguing, fighting, negativity, discord, mistrust, discontent, and jealousy.

We *need* to pray. We *have* to pray. Prayer is spiritual warfare. We must be prayer warriors. We must fight for our families through prayer. Prayer activates the powers of heaven against the forces of hell—pushing back the darkness. Prayer is our offense, and our defense, against the attacks of the evil one.

Third, we must pray because we know that God sees the bigger picture. God can see what we cannot see. God knows the future. He knows things we do not know. Even when we are in a season in our lives when everything seems great and everything is running smoothly, we do not know what is right around the corner. But God does.

It is especially important to pray when things are going well, before things have been set in motion by the enemy and things begin to fall apart. When things in our families fall apart we usually start praying for things that we wish would not have happened. We pray that somehow we could change the past, but it is too late to change some things. This is why the time to pray is always *now*. Whether things are good or bad, prayer is our preparation for what we *do not know.*

Fourth, we pray because we want the favor of God on our families. Prayer is a very personal act between an individual and God. For many years I have prayed for the favor of God on my family.

Nearly 20 years ago, a book came out called, *The Prayer of Jabez.* This book really affected me. It was based on 1 Chronicles 4:10. *"And Jabez called on the Lord God of Israel saying, 'Oh that you would bless me indeed, that you would enlarge my territory, that your hand would be with me, that you would keep me from evil, that I might not cause pain."* God granted him what he requested.

I started praying this prayer daily. That God would bless me. That God would enlarge my territory. That God would be with me. That God would keep me from sin or evil so I would not hurt anyone. This prayer has been part of my life ever since. Now, I am a Baptist, but when I pray this prayer it definitely brings out my Pentecostal side. It may seem odd to some of us to ask God to favor us. But it is Biblical. I want the favor of God for me and for my family, so I ask Him for His blessings on us. God loves when we pray to Him. He loves when we are intentional in asking for His blessings. We never bother God in our requests. He can't get enough of our seeking His favor.

I ask Him to enlarge my territory. I ask that His hand will be with me. I also spend a lot of time asking God to keep me from evil. "Lord, do not let me fall into sin, because that is going to hurt my family. I do not want to hurt those I love or cause them pain." When I finish my prayer I claim it in faith. I say to the Lord, "God, I do not know Jabez, but I believe that you answered His prayers. So Lord I'm asking you to answer my prayers."

It is important to know why we pray.

When it comes down to it, the details of how we pray do not matter. What matters is that we *intentionally* and *regularly* pray. What matters is that we know we need to pray over everything, and we do it. We have to spend time with God. Are we praying for our families? Or are we just thinking about praying for our families?

Many people have heard of John and Charles Wesley. They were the founders of the Methodist movement and preached many sermons and wrote many of our beloved hymns. You may or may not have heard of their mother, Susanna Wesley. She was the 25th of 25 children. Yes, you read that right. She grew up well educated in a preacher's home in the late 17th century. At the age of nineteen, she married Samuel Wesley, an Anglican minister, in 1688. Together they had 19 children. Eight died in childbirth. One died shortly after birth, accidentally smothered by a nurse. Ten children lived—including John and Charles.

History tells us that Samuel was a preacher, but not a great one. He spent 39 years in a church, but did not necessarily do a good job. He was not good with money, and he spent many months in a debtor's prison while trying to raise his children.

The parsonage that he lived in was on a small farm. Samuel was not the rugged, nature-loving type of man. He did not like to get his hands dirty. Therefore, Susanna and the ten children had to run the place. Susanna taught herself how to farm, and then taught her children. She taught her girls how to read, which was unheard of more than 300 years ago. She worked hard, and taught her children to do the same.

While Samuel spent most of his days writing exegetical treaties about the suffering of Job, the rest of the family physically worked hard, often suffering. Susanna did everything she could to run and organize her household so that everything that needed to be done for their livelihood was managed well. She even scheduled her time with her children, spending one hour with a different child every day, according to a planned rotation. She taught her children academics. The children had a list of chores to do every day and Susanna made sure everything went according to her planning.

She was an amazing woman.

How was she able to do all of this? Susanna spent two hours reading her Bible and praying for her family every day. They did not live in a large house. In fact, it was said to be very small. Finding a way to spend uninterrupted time with God was hard for Susanna. Children were constantly underfoot. There was constantly something trying to steal her attention. But Susanna would take her apron and pull it over her head. The children knew that when mom had her apron over her head, that was her time with the Lord. For two hours every day they would hear Susanna reading her Bible and praying for her family.

It was this faithfulness to prayer and reading Scripture that gave her the strength to manage her life. She devoted her time to God because she knew she had to rely on God's strength to get through her hard days. When she was overwhelmed with the difficulties of life, the never ending work, and the uncertainty of the future, she knew that she could find her peace, comfort, and power from time with her loving Savior.

And she taught her children by her example.

We need prayer. Our families need prayer. We need the guidance from our Savior. We need the power and strength that only comes from Him. We have to stay grounded in our relationship with Christ to be able to be the people that God has called us to be. And we do this through prayer.

CHAPTER EIGHT

// It's Time to Pray

NEXT, IT IS important to know *when* to pray for our families. First Thessalonians 5:17 says, *"Pray without ceasing."* It is important to pray when our children are young. It is important to pray when our children are growing older. It is important to pray when our children are teenagers. Pray without ceasing. This really makes more sense to us as our children gain independence and we have less control over what they are doing. We worry about them. We need to be in continual prayer for our wives. For our husbands. For our parents. So how do we pray without ceasing? There are four times every day that we can and should remember to pray.

First, we should pray before meals. We have lost the practice and discipline of praying at meal times, whether at home or at restaurants. Often we think we are too busy to pray. Meal times are a great time to pause and talk to God. We should pray before we eat. If we practice this, eventually the two will just naturally go together.

When I was a teenager, long before I met my wife, I dated a girl who invited me over to her house for Thanksgiving dinner. I was very nervous. I grew up in a strict, independent Baptist home and she also came from a strict Christian home. I do not think her parents appreciated the fact that she brought a date to dinner. She had a big family. They were all very religious and her Pawpaw prayed before Thanksgiving dinner. My theory is, since I was there, he decided to show off with a very long prayer. He prayed and he prayed and he prayed. By the time he finished it seemed like the stuffing was moldy.

The mealtime prayer does not have to be long and drawn out. It is not the time when we have to pray for every request on our prayer list. We can offer a simple prayer of thanks to God for providing food for us. We can acknowledge His provision and love for us and take the time to thank Him. It is a good way to get the whole family involved, taking turns praying.

A second way to add prayer to our lives is to pray over decisions and crisis. When we have family decisions to make, big or small, we should cover them in prayer. Any family need is a prayer need. When there is a crisis, our first reaction should be to pray. Prayer is not a last resort but a *first response.*

One day I had my girls in the car and an ambulance went by. One of the girls asked me, "Daddy, are you going to lead us in a prayer?" I had no idea what they were talking about. But I found out that my wife did this frequently with my two girls when they were young. Whenever an ambulance would drive by, they would stop and pray for the people who were in the ambulance. So like a good dad, I told them that it was my idea for mommy to do that.

I prayed with the girls.

A third time we should pray is during our daily quiet time. It is important to have our families in our prayers every day in our quiet time with God. We need to pray for our collective needs on a regular basis. I have a list I go through for my family, something for each day of the week. I pray for specific things on different days. By the end of each week I have specifically—and intentionally—prayed for all aspects of my family's life.

A fourth time we can pray is at night before we sleep. We can do this on our own. It is also a wonderful habit to teach our children, especially when they are young. Praying with our children when we tuck them in at night is a great way to get them in the habit of praying every night. It gets harder to do with our children when they are older, but we can instill the importance of talking to God. When my children became teenagers, everyone in the family went to bed at different times. Everyone had different schedules in the evenings. It would have been impossible to stick to a scheduled prayer time with them. But we hoped and prayed that what we had taught them about prayer when they were small would become their own prayer time as they grew older. We tried to set them up for success by buying them Bibles and devotional books to use. We told them we loved them and trusted them and encouraged them to walk with God on their own.

When our children were little, some of my sweetest memories were when we would tuck them in each night. My daughter, Savana, had a waterbed. We had one of the old-fashioned ones. Not one of the fancy motionless ones. We would sit the kids on the bed and watch them move back and forth with the flow of the bed. It was a full ocean hurricane sometimes. It was a lot of fun for our girls. My wife, Sherry, would eventually lay the girls down, and they would sing songs together, reads books together, and read the Bible. When they were done, they would pray. Such great memories. As children grow older it becomes more difficult to do this, so we should make these memories while we can, for the good of our families.

Sometimes it feels like our families are falling apart. We feel like we are failing at parenting. We do not know how to communicate with one another. Our marriages are struggling. Our finances are a mess. The details may differ, but our families are coming unglued. There is hope. There is a solution. The glue that can repair our families is the Word of God. The Bible gives us many practical ideas, practices, and principles that have the power to repair the areas that are broken in our families.

Healing in our families begins with prayer. I will say without reservation that prayer is the primary glue that will put our families back together. When we petition our Lord and Savior for help with our struggles, miracles can happen, even in the midst of uncertainty and feeling helpless. I often feel helpless in the life of my family, like I'm not sure what path to take. What choice should I make? What decision is best?

The pressure is so great sometimes. Especially on days like Mother's Day. How can I find that special gift that shows the mother of my children how valued and loved she is? How can we best show honor to the mothers in our lives? Sunday Brunch? Massage or manicure? Overnight getaway? I recently saw an article in which mothers told us the worst Mother's Day gifts they were ever given. Among these gifts were things like a can of beans, an ironing board cover, a calculator, toilet paper (maybe that was the same guy who gave the beans), hair dye, salad dressing, a fire extinguisher, and deodorant. We all can agree that they are ridiculous gifts. We aren't *that* bad. But what IS the best gift we can give to those we honor, love, and care for? I would suggest that the best gift we have to give one another is PRAYER. But not just the superfluous activity that we get around to when it is convenient.

Prayer is an essential part of our Christian life. Prayer is an intentional and vital part of our walk with God. Prayer is a central piece of the Christian experience. We cannot be in relationship with Christ if we are not talking to Him. And not just by saying a quick prayer before a meal. But really talking to Him about our lives, our needs, our decisions, our choices. We should want His input and we should ask Him for direction. Earlier we learned that in order to be effective parents we need to spend time with our kids. This is true of our relationship with our Heavenly Father. He longs to spend time with us.

Our families need prayer. We need to be praying for ourselves, in whatever role we play in our families. We need to be praying for one another, our spouse and our children and our grandchildren and our parents. If we are single, we should be praying for our future families.

I recently did a survey and asked my church if you could go back in time and tell your younger self one thing to do differently in life what would it be? A great number of people answered that they would tell their younger self to pray *more*. You see, we are not going to get to the end of our lives and wish we had prayed less. We are not going to be on our death beds regretting all of the time we spent in intimate communion with our Savior. We need to pray not just more often, but more intentionally.

So often, we pray only in reaction to circumstances and situations. When our marriages are falling apart, we turn to prayer. When our kids are going through a rebellious stage, we pray. We react to bad circumstances in our lives with prayer. Now, this is not a bad thing. We can and should call on the name of our Lord in times of distress, uncertainty, and despair. But prayer for our families should not only be *reactionary*. It should also be *precautionary*. We need to be praying for our marriages when they are at their strongest. We need to be praying for our children when they are being obedient and respectful. We need to be praying for our physical, mental, emotional, and spiritual health when we feel like we are at the top of the world. These are precautionary prayers. Instead of praying after things begin to fall apart, we should pray *before* they begin to fall apart.

CHAPTER NINE

// Margins, Margins

DO YOU REMEMBER writing a term paper in high school or college? When we wrote a paper, we were told there had to be *margins* on each of the pages. Most instructors called for one-inch margins around the whole page.

Did you know that when we put one-inch margins all the way around a sheet of paper, we automatically take away 37.4% of writing space? This means that more than one third of the paper is blank. If we double-space our typing, that means that more than 50% of the page is blank space. There is blank space along the perimeter of the page, between the lines on the page, and between the words on the page.

What would happen if we took out all of the blank space? The page would look very different—chaotic even. It would be cluttered, disorganized, and difficult—if not impossible—to read. Stressful, right? Reading would not be as enjoyable or even really possible if the pages were margin-less. Actually, the New Testament was originally written that way in the original Greek, with no margins or spacing. This is why it is often difficult to translate it into other languages.

So, what does this have to do with our families? I think it relates because in today's world, the average American family is living life without margins. We are cramming every second of every day with activity. We have no time or space for building relationships with others. And because of that, we have no time for love. We have no time for instructing our children. We have no time for leisure. We have no time for rest. We have no time for spiritual things in life, such as prayer, Bible study, and church.

We have an enemy who wants us to fail in every aspect of our lives—especially when it comes to our families. If the devil cannot turn us away from our relationship from God, he will settle for making us very busy, therefore distracting us from our relationship with God. The devil's sole purpose is to destroy us and our relationship with God, and he will use any means necessary to achieve his plan.

The purpose of sin in our lives is to disconnect us from our relationship with God. Sin literally separates us from God. The devil does not care about us. He does not care about our sin. He is not enamored by our sin. The only reason the enemy is introducing us to sin is to sever our relationship with God, because he hates God. His motivation is to take what God loves.

That is us.

And if he cannot get us to sin, he will try to distract us with the busy-ness of life, which can also destroy our relationships with God. Most people will not fall victim to the devil's temptation to do scandalous things, such as having an affair. But the devil can tempt us with success and a busy schedule to draw our attention, focus, and devotion to God.

Most Christians believe in following the ten commandments. And many of us do a pretty good job following them. We do not break the major rules very often. The enemy knows this. Instead, he wants to distract us with busyness, which often accomplishes the same thing as sin. It harms our relationship with God.

When we do not have a margin in our lives—a defense against the busyness—our stress increases. Without margin, our relationship intimacy decreases. Without margin, we never find time to relax and rest. Without margin, we live only to do what has to get done, instead of doing what we want to do. Without margin, our time off is not ever really time off.

This constant state of *dis-ease* is destroying our families. The problem is not a lack of love. Struggling families often love one another greatly. The problem is that we do not have margin, which helps us to exercise our priorities.

There are three factors that help us to define margin. First, margin is the space between our *load* and our *limit*. The limit to our load should be higher than our actual load. The space between the load and our limit is the space where we get to relax, to breathe, to prioritize, to enjoy life, and to enjoy one another. The closer our load gets to the limit that we can handle, the less time and resources we have to enjoy our lives. The less energy we have to develop relationship and intimacy with our loved ones. The closer our load is to the limit we can handle, the higher our stress and anxiety levels.

Second, margin is the space available beyond what is necessary in our lives. There are always certain things we must do. We must work. We must sleep. We must eat. We must take care of our responsibilities. If our responsibilities in life are more than what is necessary, that marginal space gets smaller and smaller. We have less time and energy to do things that should be priorities for us.

I get up every morning around 5:30 A.M. Recently, I bought a stainless steel coffee percolator on *Amazon* for about $30. My routine is to wake up early, turn the percolator on, wait the 30 minutes for the coffee to be ready, and then proceed to drink a pot of coffee every morning. One Sunday morning, I got up, turned the percolator on, got dressed, did a few things I needed to do, then finally went and filled my cup with coffee. I walked to my office, sat down to go over my sermon for church that day, lifted the coffee to my mouth and proceeded to pour it on my shirt. You see, I had failed to realize that I had filled the cup too high—to the brim of the cup. There was no space for the coffee to go when I began tilting it toward my mouth.

That's coffee without margin.

Third, margin is the ability to add to something without causing overflow. Many of us find ourselves in a place in life when one more drop of coffee is going to send us over the edge. One more drop is going to put us over the top. We are one drop away from breakdown.

We need margin.

There are three areas in our family lives that need margin. Developing space in these three areas will help us to have successful families and happy homes. First, we must have margin in our *finances*. The book of Proverbs is full of wisdom that is applicable to our daily lives. Proverbs 13:7 says, *"One person pretends to be rich but has nothing. Another pretends to be poor but has abundant wealth."* This proverb seems simple enough. It describes two different people. One person pretends to have more than he really does. He is living above his means. There is no margin in his life. His load and limit are right next to each other. One more financial "drop of coffee" could send them over the edge.

Most Americans live paycheck to paycheck. Credit cards have made it easy to spend more than we earn. Therefore, many families are one emergency away from losing everything. We pretend to be rich, but in reality we have very little assurance and security. Even when we get a raise and make more money, we immediately spend it. We always want bigger, better, and newer. When we spend what we take in, we leave no room for margin. When there is no margin we are always on the verge of trouble.

The Proverb says that the person who pretends to be rich has nothing. I would like to disagree with this for a moment, because the person who pretends to be rich does have something. He has stress. He has anxiety. He has worry. He may look wealthy from afar, but if we look closely we see that, behind the scenes, all he has is insecurity.

The second person pretends to be poor. In reality he simply is living on less than he earns. He is living below his means. This is rare in our American culture. But the Bible tells us that when we live comfortably below what we earn, we feel rich. Living below our means, or living with financial margin in our lives, means that something unexpected can happen without it causing a financial catastrophe in our lives. A medical emergency, a car repair, a broken water heater, a root canal, or braces. We can be prepared for the unexpected and the inevitable when we live with financial margin.

It is often uncomfortable to discuss money. But it is so important to have a Godly and healthy relationship with our finances. When Jesus walked this earth, 16 of 38 of His parables were about money and possessions. Nearly one fourth of Jesus's words recorded in the New Testament deal with Biblical stewardship or money. One out of ten verses in the gospels refers to money. In fact, there are more than 2,000 verses in the Bible about tithing, money, and possessions. Money is mentioned in Scripture twice as much as faith and prayer combined.

God cares about our relationship with money.

He knows that if we are not good stewards of our money, spending more than we earn, that our family is going to be filled with stress. We will face anxiety, worry, and hurt when our finances are out of control and unmanageable. Often in our households, there is one spouse who is stressed about money and one who does not know about the family's money problems, so this person keeps spending in an unhealthy manner. The one who pays the bill becomes resentful of the free spender, but still does not talk about it. So not only is there financial disarray, but there are also marital problems.

So what can we do to create financial margin in our lives? First, a *budget* is a practical solution to this problem. Families need to work together on planning a budget. A budget helps a family know the amount of money that is coming in and how much is going out. So make a budget. Stick to a budget. Putting it in writing helps us to face the reality of our financial situation, instead of burying our heads in the sand like we often do.

Second, we can *downsize* and downgrade. Dave Ramsey has a lot to say on this subject. Get a smaller house, a cheaper house, an older car. Americans are drowning in debt because they think they are entitled to what they cannot truly afford.

Third, we can cut out some recurring expenses that are not necessary. We can downgrade our cable or satellite programming. We can give up certain subscriptions that we can live without. The little monthly expenses that do not seem that important add up to a lot of money each month.

Fourth, we can aggressively pay down debt—especially consumer debt. This takes sacrifice. The money that we would spend eating out at restaurants goes a long way to paying off debt. The money for lattes from the coffee shop goes a long way towards paying off debt. Instead of going out for date night, get creative and save money by staying in and put that money towards debt. We should do everything we can to pay off our debt.

Fifth, we can find *extra income*. We can get a part-time job. We can sell household items on the internet. We can find creative ways to make extra money. Then, use the extra income to pay down debt.

We are spending ourselves into financial ruin because of want. We must be honest with ourselves about what is actually needed, and what is simply wanted. Wanting something does not mean we are entitled to it if we do not have the money for it. So we take an honest look at it and ask ourselves, "What can we live without?"

I have a confession to make. I love watches. I am guilty of buying way more watches than a person requires. I also love shoes. I have more shoes than my wife does. Every time we go to a department store I love walking through the shoe section. I love electronics. I want everything at *Best Buy*. But I do not *need* any of these things. I simply want them. I have to be careful, because I can turn a want into a need. I can rationalize my want and talk myself into thinking that it is something I need.

If we are being honest, we all do this at times. My daughter recently told me that they needed a television for their house. My initial reaction was to save the day and give them one of our televisions, knowing that I would then "need" to buy a new one to replace it. I turned a want into a need. I masked it with the motivation of helping my daughter. But really I just wanted a better and newer television and this was just the excuse I could use to get it.

Finally, once we get our spending and our debt under control, we should strive to live off 70% of our income. With the other 30% we tithe, save, and invest.

If we are living off of 100% of our income, we are headed for trouble. We have to sit down and make a budget based on 70% of our income. I understand that is not immediately possible for some of us, because we have overstretched ourselves financially and are drowning in debt.

If this is the case then start by implementing the practices and principles I listed above. We start changing the way we view and treat money. We work toward financial health. We start paying down debt and not creating more debt. We start putting something, even if it is only a small amount, in savings.

We must start now.

There will never be an easy and ideal time to sacrifice for financial health. There will always be children, grandchildren, health problems, maintenance issues, car problems that vie for our money. We have to budget and plan and be good stewards of the finances that have been entrusted to us by God.

CHAPTER TEN

// And More Margins

THE SECOND THING we need is *moral* margin. First Thessalonians 5:22 says, *"Abstain from all appearance of evil."* Paul does not tell us to abstain from evil, but even the *appearance* of evil. In other words, we should walk so far away from the line of sin that if we fall we will not fall into sin. Moral margin is putting a safe distance between sin and ourselves. We put certain safeguards in place. We choose accountability. We do not keep secrets. We are intentional about staying far away from sin. Then, when we fall, we may break our own standards, but we are not breaking God's standards.

Adam and Eve did not have this kind of margin. The reason we have sin today is because of Adam and Eve. God told them they could eat of the fruit of every tree in the garden except for one. And what did Adam and Eve do? Did they avoid that tree? Did they take care to stay as far away from it as possible? No. They stood at the tree. They wanted to see it. To smell it. To touch it. They did not run farther from it, but stood closer to it. They did not necessarily plan to eat it, but they sure wanted to be close to it. Maybe take a whiff of it. Maybe just hold it. Their moral margin eroded until the day that they were tempted and ate it.

Like Adam and Eve, we get into trouble when our moral margin erodes. Our families fall apart when our moral margin erodes. Husbands and wives make bad decisions when their moral margin erodes. Teenagers make poor choices when their moral margin erodes. The old saying warns us not to get too close to the fire, lest we get burned. If we get too close to the edge we will fall off.

Meenakshi Moorthy and Visnu Viswanath loved adventure. In 2018, they visited the Grand Canyon and posted a picture on Instagram of them standing at the edge with this caption; "A lot of us, including yours truly, is (sic) a fan of daredevilry. Attempts at the edge of cliffs and skyscrapers, but did you know that wind gusts can be fatal? Is your life worth just one photo?" A few months later, standing on the edge of a cliff in Yosemite Park they both fell to their deaths. They were found because they had set a tripod to take a photo before a gust of wind blew them off the edge of a cliff.

When we get too close to the edge it is easier to fall.

The moral edge works like that. So how do we keep our moral edge from eroding? How do we keep our bad days from leading to bad decisions that affect our families? When families fight how do we keep our marriages from suffering?

There are four ways we can keep our moral margins from eroding.

First, husbands and wives should not keep secrets from each other. There should be transparency between spouses. We should not have social media secrets. Our phones should never be off limits to each other. We should not hide our phones, turning them face-down so our spouse cannot see the notifications. We should know each others' passwords. If we have to hide something, there is something we should not be doing. There can be no secrets in healthy relationships. We are as sick as our secrets.

Second, we must build safe boundaries. We need to build boundaries in our relationships that not only help us to avoid sin, but help us to avoid the road to sin.

Third, for our family's sake, we should always be guarded with the opposite sex; in our actions as well as in our words. We should not be talking to anyone more than our spouse. We should not be talking about our spouse to someone of the opposite sex. We should not be sharing parts of our heart and mind with someone of the opposite sex; that should be reserved for our spouses. This means no complaining to coworkers or with online friends about our marriages. No sharing with the opposite sex that we are not getting along with our spouse. This is the beginning of tragedy in our lives. Therefore we must build a code of conduct into our lives that keeps us from crossing the line. Few people plan to have an affair, but when we do not put these boundaries in place we find ourselves on a slippery slope towards sin.

Fourth, we should spend time daily with God. We need to be reading His Word and growing closer to God. There is an old saying that says, "Sin will keep you from the

Bible or the Bible will keep you from sin." A daily walk with the Lord, hearing from Him through His Word, and speaking to Him in prayer, will keep us from sin. I have known many preachers over the years who have fallen into immorality. The first thing they told me was that they quit spending time with God. Their relationship with God was not important to them. Without our living and growing relationship with Christ, we are vulnerable to falling, and destroying everything we love.

We need *moral margin* in our lives.

The third thing we need is *calendar* margin. Ephesians 5:16 says, *"Making the most of the time because the days are evil."* What does this mean? It means that our days have a way of getting away from us. We stay busy without accomplishing anything of importance. How many of us have ever had a long day? When one of our loved ones asks us how our day went we may answer that it was very busy from morning to night. We are then asked, "What did you do?" Often we cannot come up with a satisfactory answer of what we accomplished in all that busyness.

We spend our days going nonstop, but yet we accomplish very little. Hours roll into days. Days roll into months. Months roll into years. Years roll into a lifetime. At the end of it all, we often cannot say what we accomplished. We can only say we did a lot of it and we were very busy doing it. We move at high speed, no matter our stage in life. Newlyweds. New parents. Empty nesters. Grandparents. We never slow down. We need to add calendar margin into our lives.

How do we do this?

First, we have to understand that there is an ebb and flow to our lives. Some times will be busier than others, by nature. For example, new parents have full days and nights, always going, rarely sleeping. I remember when my daughters were young it seemed like I went many years without getting a good night's sleep. But these times pass. And there is a bit of a reprieve. Then the busyness of the next cycle of life starts. This is the ebb and flow of life.

Second, we must prioritize. We must be intentional about putting what is important to us first. If family is important then we have to make sure we make time for it first, before all else. If we are not intentional about prioritizing, the important things will pass right by us.

Third, we have to get done what we *have to* get done, so we have time to do what we *want to* do. So we must work hard to take care of our responsibilities in a timely fashion. Procrastination only makes us suffer later.

Fourth, we must *calendar* important things. Date night with your spouse. Quality time with our children. Family meals. Put it on the calendar, like an appointment. And when something else comes up we must say, "I'm sorry, I have an appointment with my family." We have to make time for these things. Time passes. Our children's childhoods pass. We do not want to miss these moments.

Fifth, we should take vacations. And we should not bring our work with us! We need a vacation from the busyness of life; when we can simply be with our families, enjoying the moments. Work can wait. Even when we have too much work and we have stress at work, it is important to prioritize time away with our families. Work will be there when we get back.

Sixth, we have to learn to say no to things—even good things. If life was about saying no to bad things and yes to good things it would be simple. But it is not. Often, we are faced with the temptation to say yes to more good things than we have time for. We cannot be all things for all people. Calendar margin means we sometimes have to say no to the good things in order to say yes to the best things.

Seventh, we need to remember that every day is a clean slate. We often expect perfection from ourselves. We cannot expect to do more than we have the ability to do. So we should get done what we can get done in a day, and then be prepared for the next day.

Eighth, we should rise early. If you are a night person you hate hearing that. But if we rise earlier in the day, creating a routine, we tend to get more done during the day. So take a shower, make a pot of coffee and make it a priority to rise early. I sometimes put my alarm clock across the room so that I have to get out of bed to shut it off.

Ninth, we should limit digital distractions. Many of us spend the day buried in our phones without accomplishing anything. Our phones distract us from what is important. If we want quality time with our family, we should put our phones aside. A great tip is to put it in a basket during family time. Walk away from it. We need to show our families that they are more important than whatever it is on the screen that tries to distract us. Most of us have been at a restaurant and have seen a family sitting at a table, every single one of them looking at their phones instead of talking to each other. This is so sad. We need to limit distractions so that our families know they are important to us.

Tenth, we need to serve the Lord together. We should make time for church as a family. Serving and worshipping God as a family must be a priority; not something we do if we have the time.

Finally, we need to realize that we do not have it as bad as we think we do. We talk about how stressed and busy we are. How things used to be much simpler when we were young. There seemed to be more time. We seemed to be less busy. However, this simply is not true. Research shows that we have just as much free time as Andy Griffith had many years ago. We are simply wasting our free time. In America, our busyness is a measure of success, yet it brings anxiety into our hearts and lives, and, by default, our families.

When we prioritize our responsibilities, concentrate on what is important to us, and bring margin into our lives, we can free our lives of the stress and anxiety that comes when we feel too busy. We will have room to breathe. We will control our schedule, rather than having our schedule controlling us.

God does not want us to be stressed and anxious. He wants us to find our rest in Him. He promises to give us rest, but we have to be willing to work hard and do our part, instead of just staying in the rat race and complaining about how busy and stressed we are. When we stay this way we are hurting our families. We are not teaching our children a better way to live.

According to John Gordon, we cannot be stressed and thankful at the same time. It is emotionally impossible to be thankful and stressed at the same time. So when we are feeling stressed, we should intentionally choose to practice gratitude instead.

Some seasons of life will be busier than others. When my girls were younger there was one year that they were on different basketball teams. During that year they participated in 87 basketball games. That number did not include practices or tournaments or trips. That was a crazy and busy year. We complained about it often. But then we had a shift in attitude, realizing that one day it would all be over, and we would wish we had a game to go to. We would love to see our girls play again. We learned to appreciate the moments, even when we were tired and rushed. We did not want our girls to only have memories of our complaining about their schedule. We wanted them to know that we valued what was important to them, and we loved to see them play. We stopped complaining about being busy and stressed, practiced gratitude, and the result was that we enjoyed our lives much more.

So enjoy the crazy ride of life. If we implement financial, moral, and calendar margin in our lives, it is possible.

CHAPTER ELEVEN

// How To Ruin Your Life By 25

WHEN WE FEEL like our families are coming unglued, the Bible gives us practical advice for making our families stick. Even if they fall apart, the Bible is the glue that can put us back together again.

Twenty-five years of counseling, the application of common sense, and study of God's Word have taught me many things that I wish I had understood when I was first starting out in life. There are many Godly principles that lead to success, especially when implemented when we are young. They are applicable at any age, of course, but learning these things at a younger age will help us avoid some of the traps, pitfalls, temptations, and troubles that the enemy uses to throw us off track. So if you are young, please pay particular attention.

In January of 2019, the Dutch Defense Safety Inspection Agency launched an investigation into an F-16 that was shot while it was on a training exercise. When the pilot was able to land the jet, they discovered that rounds had passed through both the engine and the fuselage. The courageous pilot was fortunate to avoid a crash.

This particular F-16 jet was equipped with a Vulcan Gatling gun that is capable of firing 6,000 rounds of ammunition per minute. Those rounds travel at a velocity of 3,450 feet per second. Now, I'm not a math genius but, if I've done my math correctly, that calculates to over a half mile per second! That is fast!

As they were investigating the shots that were fired on that F-16 while it was in mid-air, they realized that the plane actually had shot itself. When the F-16 hits turbo speed it flies faster than 3,450 feet per second. The pilot had literally shot his own gun and was then hit by his own rounds.

Most people have heard the phrase, "He shot himself in the foot." It means that we make a situation worse for ourselves. We demonstrate gross incompetence. The pilot figuratively shot himself in the foot when he shot himself in the engine.

This is human nature. We often make things worse for ourselves and "shoot ourselves in the foot." The book of Proverbs is a book that is designed to keep us from flying into our own bullets. It aims to keep us from shooting ourselves in the foot. It helps keep us away from making mistakes that can be avoided. It gets us out of our own way. If we heed the warnings in Proverbs, they will keep us on a healthy path, a prosperous path, a Godly path, a blessed path. And if we learn these lessons while we are young, we will avoid ruining our lives so that we can live the lives God intends us to live.

The book of Proverbs offers words of wisdom to build our lives upon. It is a recalibration of our daily lives. There are thirty one days in most months. And there are thirty one chapters in the book of Proverbs. I do not think this is a coincidence. I was given advice many years ago to read a chapter of Proverbs every day. There is wisdom, direction, and strength to be found in this daily reading.

I will highlight ten themes pulled from ten verses found in the book of Proverbs that will help us to live prosperous lives.

Fear the Lord

Proverbs 1:7 says, *"The fear of the Lord is the beginning of knowledge but fools despise wisdom and instruction."* According to commentators, this verse sets the tone for the whole book of Proverbs. Fear of the Lord. According to this verse, knowledge, wisdom, and blessing all begin with acknowledging that God is, and that He is God.

When we fear the Lord, we listen to His instruction. When we fear the Lord, we respect and regard the Bible. When we fear the Lord, we submit to His Word. We submit to His will. We submit to His ways. A fool despises the Lord in His wisdom. It is crazy to ignore God's will and His ways. We can save ourselves a lot of trouble and heartache if we just revere, respect, and fear His Word. Often we do not understand God's reasons for asking something of us, just as a raw recruit doesn't understand the reasons behind their instructions while in training. But we learn that if the Bible says to do something, that means that God has a reason and a purpose for it. If the Bible says not to do something, we will be blessed if we avoid doing it. And understanding will eventually come.

God's reasons are Holy. His intentions are pure. His commands are not there to enslave us, to keep us from having fun, to ruin our lives. His commands are there to protect us, to direct us, and to bless us. Everything He does is out of love. God is the author and architect of life. He knows what brings prosperity. He knows what brings success. He knows the bigger picture. After all, He designed and created everything and everyone. His instruction saves us from ourselves, our sinful will, and an immediate and future misery.

Our human will often resists this. We focus on the "thou shalt nots" and we often think that following God's ways will leave us with a boring and miserable life. But the Bible tells us that there is only pleasure in sin for a little bit of time. The devil makes sin look attractive to us, and there can, in fact, be pleasure. But God knows what is best for us. He keeps the long view in mind. He tells us that the temporary pleasure of sin will pass and will leave us with a lifetime of misery. We are blessed when we obey God.

Proverbs 3:5–6 says, *"Trust in the Lord with all your heart and lean not on your own understanding. In all your ways acknowledge Him and He shall direct your paths."* I recently asked my church to fill out a survey. One of the questions asked "if you could go back in time and tell yourself one thing after you graduated high school, what would you say to yourself?" The overwhelming majority of people answered that they would tell their younger self to keep Jesus Christ number one in their lives. To make relationship with Him and obedience to Him the top priority. To keep Christ at the center of everything. To focus on Christ. These people have lived full lives. They have experienced the ups and downs, the good and the bad; they have made mistakes and seen success, and have figured out what is most important. It would be wise to heed their suggestions. It starts with centering our lives around Christ and fearing the Lord.

Tithe

Proverbs 3:9-10 says, *"Honor the Lord with your with your possessions and with the first fruit of all your increase."* Why? *"So your barns would be filled with plenty, and your vats will overflow with new wine."* By the way, new wine in the Bible is grape juice. But I will get to that later.

In the Bible, first fruits always refers to the tithe that belongs to the Lord. The tithe is the first ten percent of the income. God is saying that the tithe is to be given to the Lord before anything else is given to him. It does not matter how little or how much we make. If you make $1,000 per week, you tithe. If you work part time at Chick-fil-a and only make $40 per week, you tithe. Here's why. When we tithe, we honor the Lord. When we do not tithe, we take the blessings of the Lord for granted. When we do not tithe off income, we are saying to God, "I deserve this, not You."

God does not actually need our money. Tithing is not simply the church needing money. Tithing is more about our hearts. My wife and I have been blessed in our lives. I believe it is because we have always honored God with the first fruits of our income. We are not wealthy by any stretch of the imagination. But we have all that we need and more. We have honored God by willingly giving back just a small portion of what He gives us, and because of that, we are blessed beyond what we deserve.

The amount is not what is important. In fact, it is often harder to tithe when we have less income. It may be easier to tithe off of a $4,000 paycheck than a $400 paycheck, where every penny is important when it is time to pay the bills. But here is what I have learned, if we aren't obedient with little, we will not be obedient with a lot. We often say, "When I am more financially stable, or when I make more money, THEN I will tithe. But if we don't tithe with the $400 paycheck, we won't be willing to tithe off the $4,000 paycheck. If we don't tithe with the $4,000 income, we won't tithe with a $40,000 paycheck. If we don't tithe with a $40,000 paycheck we will not tithe even if we make $4,000,000.

Why is that? Because it is not about the money. It's the principle of honoring God. We have a hard time understanding this. Later is never a good time to tithe. The time is always now. Waiting until we have enough money is not honoring to God. Because tithing is not about money. Tithing is about the heart. The Bible tells us to honor the Lord with our finances all of the days of our life. Proverbs 22:9 says, *"He who has a generous eye will be blessed."* No matter our financial situation, no matter our net worth, no matter how much debt we have, no matter our fears, the time to tithe is now.

Choose Friends Carefully

This is a great principle for young people to learn. Proverbs 4:14–15 says, "Do not enter the path of the wicked and do not walk in the way of evil." Do not travel on it. Avoid it. Turn away from it. We are going to have opportunities in life to make friends. We are going to be invited into situations that do not honor God. We are going to be tempted with things that go against what God wants for us. We will be exposed to things that seem fun, exciting, and enticing. Often our friends will invite us into these situations: parties, alcohol, drugs, sex. The wrong friends will even be cheering us on as we are faced with these things, encouraging us to do the wrong thing.

No matter what our friends are saying, do not do it. In fact, here is better advice. Get away from the situation, and even the friend. Because a real friend, a true friend, will never try to take us away from our relationship with the Lord.

Proverbs says, *"He who walks with wise men will be wise, but the companion of fools will be destroyed."* This verse does not say, "If you walk with wise men you will be wise, but if you walk with fools you will be a fool." No. When we walk with fools, we will not only be fools ourselves, but the Bible says that we will face destruction and ruin our lives. So, it is important to be careful in picking our friends, those with whom we walk. Whether in middle school, high school, college, or life, the friends we make will have an impact on our lives. Research tells us that we become who we spend time with. So if we want to live Godly, productive lives, we need to surround ourselves with people who love God and have a high degree of self-discipline and self-control.

A 2013 study published in *Psychological Science* reports that when people are running low on self-control, they often seek out self-disciplined people to boost their willpower. They also found out that friends greatly influence their choices. A

2014 study published in *The Journal of Consumer Research* found that friends often bond by providing one another moral support to resist temptation. But the opposite is also true. Other researchers have discovered that, when it came to resisting temptations, like eating chocolate, sometimes friends were more likely to become partners in crime. Rather than resisting, they indulged.

So we have to watch whom we make our friends. We need to surround ourselves with people we want to be like. Our lives will be better and we will save ourselves a lot of trouble if we find friends with the same Christian values that we have. We should be selective about the company that we keep.

CHAPTER TWELVE

// It Starts with Fearing the Lord

Be Life-Long Learners

PROVERBS 12:4 SAYS, *"Whoever loves instruction loves knowledge, but he who hates correction is stupid."* This verse teaches us two things. First, we should always be learning. To be a lifelong learner means we should love instruction and knowledge. We should always strive to make ourselves better. We can always be trying to be better Christians, better parents, better employees, better husbands and wives, better children. And we do this by continually learning.

Second, this verse instructs us to receive correction well. The Bible uses the "S" word: Stupid. When we make a mistake, we should be open to correction. We can always learn how to do things differently and better. This is what it means to be a lifelong learner.

Family Matters

Proverbs 12:4 says, *"An excellent wife is the crown of her husband, but she who causes shame is like rottenness in the bones."* The principle of this verse applies to husbands and wives. Family is for life. It is supposed to be that way. Even in broken homes and in families of divorce, we are still attached to each other in some shape or form. So when choosing a spouse, we should take care. It is not a flippant decision to be made just because we had a few fun dates. So often we get married because we love the idea of marriage. This can lead to misery.

It is important to really know someone before marrying them. Yes, there are stories from our grandparents who only knew each other for two weeks before getting married and have been married for over 50 years. But in today's culture that is the exception, not the rule. It is important to take our time to truly know a person.

Now this does not mean that we live together to get to know them before we are married. This is wrong in the eyes of God. God created marriage and He says that sex belongs only in marriage. God knows what is best for us. He wants to protect us.

In a non-Christian study, science and research show us that cohabitation, or living together without the benefit of marriage, is more stressful than being married. Often we move in together as a sort of "test drive" for marriage, with the intent of getting married eventually. But research shows that only 50% of people who live together ever get married.

And those who live together have a separation rate five times higher than those who are married. The reconciliation rate was only one third the rate of married couples. Cohabitating couples are also more likely to experience infidelity in the relationship. Compared to those waiting until marriage to live together, cohabitating couples have poor relationship quality. There are reports of more fighting and violence and less reported happiness. Cohabitating couples also earn less money and are less wealthy than their married peers. Compared to married individuals, those cohabitating have higher levels of depression and substance abuse.

If this were true of any other area of life we would avoid it like the plague. The Bible says, *"Marriage is honorable among all and the bed undefiled, but fornicators and adulterers, God will judge."* Fornication is sex outside of the marriage relationship. It is never ok in God's eyes to live together before marriage.

So choose carefully. Proverbs tells us, *"Better is a dry morsel with quietness than a house full of feasting with strife."* *"It is better to dwell in the corner of a housetop than in a house shared with a contentious woman."* Remember, this does not only apply to women. It applies to both husbands and wives. Choosing poorly hurts.

Proverbs also shows examples of choosing a spouse wisely. *"He who finds a wife finds a good thing. He obtains favor from the Lord."* So when choosing a spouse, seek counsel. Pray. Follow the Lord, not just the heart. Why can't we trust our hearts? Because the Bible says, *"Your heart is desperately wicked."* The heart can lead us astray. We can't trust our hearts to lead us in a wise direction. The heart does dumb things. Many of us can remember a time when we were younger and fell in love with someone and, looking back, we realize how crazy it was. We must follow the Lord, not the heart.

Watch What You Say

"He who guards his mouth preserves his life." "Whoever guards his mouth and tongue keeps his soul from trouble." Our mouths get us in more trouble than anything else over the course of your life. Our words affect everything. They can get us in trouble at work. They can get us in trouble with our friends. They can hurt our families. When we look back at the end of our lives, there is going to be a huge book full of words that we said and now wish we could take back. So, we should try to control our words. We should speak words that are positive and helpful. We should not gossip. We should pause before lashing out in anger. Words can hurt.

I rarely give advice from the lyrics of country music. I may give advice from 80's rock songs, but not country music. But there is one song that gives great advice. The lyrics simply say to always be humble and kind. That's good advice. We should watch what we say.

Do Not Fall Into the Trap

The oldest trap in the book is found in Proverbs 23. *"My son give me your heart and let your eyes observe my ways for a harlot is a deep pit and a seductress is a narrow well. She also lies in wait for a victim, increases the unfaithful among men. Who has woe? Who has sorrow? Who has contentions? Who has complaints? Who has wounds without cause? Who has redness of eyes? Those who linger long at the wine. Those who go in search of mixed wine. Do not look on the wine when it's red, when it sparkles in the cup, when it goes down smoothly. At the last it bites like a serpent, it stings like a viper. Your eyes will see strange things. Your heart will utter perverse things. Yes, you'll be like one who lies down in the midst of the sea or like one who lies at the top of the mast, saying they have struck me but I was not hurt. They have beaten me but I did not feel it. When will I awake that I may seek another drink?"*

The oldest trap in the book can be summed up in this way, wine and women, adultery and alcohol, sexual sin and inebriation. Some people may question whether the Bible tells us not to drink. But if we study the Bible, I believe that it is clear that we should not drink. We have to understand what wine was in Biblical times. In those days there were no refrigeration or fermentation processes like we have today. They did not have the science to make beer or hard liquor. It wasn't possible. They only made wine. They made wine and they stored it as jelly in jars. They mixed it with water in order to purify the water because the water had amoebas and bacteria in it that would make them sick. The wine purified the water so they could drink it.

That is what the Bible calls "new wine." It was stored and mixed as a paste because it did not keep for very long. Proverbs 23 tells us to not even look at wine when it makes a color in the cup. You see they would dilute the paste in the water, just enough to kill the amoebas that were in the water, but they would never drink it. Those who drank wine with color in the cup were considered apostates. The Bible says over and over again that one has to tarry long at the wine. Their wine had less than one percent alcohol content in it. They would have had to drink for days to get drunk. It was possible, but it would have taken a lot of effort. Imagine how many times they would have had to go to the bathroom?

The other part of the trap is sexual sin. The devil entices us with temptation. But we will never be happy if we commit sexual sin, whether it is sex before marriage, or adultery. It will never bring us true satisfaction and fulfillment. In fact it will bring misery and pain. I have counseled many people over the years, grown men and women who are still dealing with the emotional, spiritual, and physical consequences of sexual sin long ago, when they were young. Years later they still deal with shame and regret. People have told me that if they could go back in time and do it all differently, the way God tells us to, that they would.

Often sexual sin and inebriation go together. Alcohol weakens our defenses. It reduces our logical and rational thinking. It makes us more swayed by emotions. It creates the perfect mental state for bad decisions. Alcohol never does anything good for us. Whenever someone has a health issue and goes to the doctor, usually one of the first suggestions is to avoid alcohol. Doctors know it is not good for you, physically. And it is dangerous, not just physically, but emotionally and spiritually because it weakens us and makes us susceptible to sin, especially sexual sin.

Parents, take note. What we as parents do in moderation, our children often do in excess. Moms and dads, we need to clean our refrigerators out and remove alcohol from our homes. We want to set an example for our children.

Work Hard

Hard work never hurt anyone. Proverbs 22:13 says, *"The lazy man says 'There's a lion outside. I'll be slain in the street.'"* In other words, a lazy man will use any excuse to avoid working. Ronald Reagan used to quote Proverbs 14:23, which says, *"In all labor there is profit."*

Proverbs is full of verses that urge us to work hard and warn us against laziness. As Christians, we should work not only hard, but we should be the hardest workers around us. When it is time to work we should outshine everyone around us. We should be busy, and active. We should put our hands to the plow and do it. In our offices, in our jobs, in our homes, wherever it may be: Success follows sweat.

Do Not Do Life Alone

Proverbs 12:15 says, *"The way of a fool is right in his own eyes, but he who heeds counsel is wise."* And Proverbs 11:14 says, *"Where there is no counsel the people fall but in the multitude of counselors there is safety."* We should not make our decisions in life without Godly counsel and help. Why? Because sometimes we cannot see the forest for the trees. Sometimes our perspective is wrong, and we need insight from others who are wise. We should always seek the advice of others who know more than we do. Make sure they are people who are wise themselves and follow God's ways.

I used to be a plant manager. At one point I had as many as 60 employees working for me. I would manage by walking around on Mondays, going from station to station, asking how my employees were doing. They knew I was a

Christian and would often say that they needed prayer. They came to me for counsel because they could see that I had my life together. They didn't ask the woman who had been married seven times for martial advice. That wouldn't have helped. They asked someone who was wise and followed God's ways. Following God's ways leads to success. So we need to seek counsel from those who know what they are talking about and have something to offer.

Protect Your Reputation

Protect your name. Proverbs 22:1 says, *"A good name is to be chosen rather than great riches, loving favor more than silver or gold."* If we have a choice between a big bank account and a good character, we should choose character. We need to guard our reputations all the days of our lives. We need to remember this when we use social media, such as *Snapchat, Instagram, Facebook*. The posts and content that we put on social media are out there forever. We should never put anything on the internet that we do not want the whole world to see. We have to guard our reputations and our family name, everywhere we go and in every decision we make. If we are Christians we carry God's name with us everywhere we go, so we need to represent Him well to others. We need to honor Him in everything we do. We don't want to be the ones who give Christians a bad name, and in doing so, give Jesus a bad reputation.

In 1967, in Pittsburgh, Pennsylvania, there lived a man named Jim Delligatti. He owned twelve *McDonald's* franchises. He was concerned and reported to headquarters that *Big Boy* and *Burger King* were beating him in hamburger sales. He suggested that they needed something to liven up the hamburger market and he had an idea. He had developed a new type of hamburger. Corporate did not like the idea at first and kept telling him no. But he persisted. Jim Delligatti, in his 12 stores, introduced something that we now call a *Big Mac*. By 1969, it accounted for nineteen percent of *McDonald's* worldwide sales. The company, even today, sells 550 million *Big Macs* per year. In 2007, they erected a *Big Mac* museum in Pittsburgh with a fourteen-foot-tall Big Mac. This sandwich, with two all beef patties, special sauce, lettuce, cheese, pickles, onions, on a sesame seed bun, is famous.

One would think that Jim Dellgatti would be a rich man because of his idea and persistence. It changed the trajectory of the future of *McDonalds*. If he had gotten any type of royalty he would be rich. In 2007, he was interviewed and was asked, "How much money did you get from the Big Mac?" He answered, "I got a plaque." He invented the most famous food in American history and he got a plaque.

We can protect our name and have good character. We may not make millions. We may not even get a plaque. But we will receive rewards in heaven.

It starts with fearing the Lord.

Epilogue

SO, NOW YOU know what God's Word says about making your family stick. The question is, "when should you start implementing these things in your life?" RIGHT NOW! IMMEDIATELY! Why would you waste another moment of your life not experiencing the fullness of the relationship with your spouse and your children that God intended?

I encourage you to call your spouse and invite them on a date. Make all the arrangements—the babysitter, the reservations. And when you get to the restaurant, put down your phones and talk. Really talk. Maybe start off by simply asking, "How was your day?" And really listen to the answer. Then, do this on a regular basis.

I also encourage you to plan a playdate with your kids. It doesn't matter if they are babies, middle schoolers, in college, or all grown up and out on their own. Spend some time doing something fun with them. Maybe go to the park, go fishing, or take them to a ball game. And while you're with them—encourage them. Let them know how awesome you think they are and how proud you are of them. Promise yourself that this will be a nag-free playdate and focus on being their biggest cheerleader.

I'm not suggesting that once you start doing the things outlined in this book you will automatically and always have the perfect marriage and perfect relationship with your kids. I'm not suggesting that at all. You will still have fights and problems. But by applying God's Word, you can fight better. (Remember, a soft answer . . .) You can learn the contentment of giving in, even when you know you're right, for the sake of the relationship.

Your kids are a reflection of you, so work at being a better person in order to be a better parent. Kids need to know that mom and dad love each other, and that the marriage relationship takes priority. If you are teaching your kids to follow the Bible, make sure you are following the Bible yourself. Take your kids to church with you every week. Talk with them about the sermons you've heard or Scripture you've read. Tell them about the great things you've seen God do. Pray together, serve together, worship together. Let them see you tithe—help them to figure money out. Remember, they are going to grow up and move out one day, and it's your job to help them make a healthy transition into adulthood.

One of the most important things you can do for your spouse and for your kids is to pray. If you aren't praying for your family, then who is? Pray when things are going good and pray when things are going bad. Pray intentionally and regularly. Pray without ceasing.

Don't be too hard on yourself if you fall short. We serve a God that is full of mercy and grace. Remember that every day is a clean slate.

Stay in God's Word and keep talking with Him. No matter what our struggle, Scripture can point us to the love and power of God—to glue it all back together.

Websites Consulted for This Book

https://www.happify.com/hd/the-science-behind-a-happy-relationship/

https://www.daveramsey.com/pr/money-ruining-marriages-in-america

https://www.thedailybeast.com/divorce-stats-that-can-predict-your-marriages-success?ref=scroll

https://www.inc.com/melanie-curtin/science-says-happy-couples-have-these-13- characteristics.html

https://www.mckinleyirvin.com/family-law-blog/2015/august/surprising-stats-on-social-media- divorce-infogra/

http://www.foryourmarriage.org/blogs/does-religious-devotion-or-lack-thereof-affect- marriages-and-families/

https://www.preachingtoday.com/illustrations/2019/april/hollywood-actors-arrested-in-college-admissions-fraud.

https://www.todaysparent.com/family/strong-parental-relationships-build-happy-children/

https://www.bakadesuyo.com/2013/10/how-to-have-a-happy-family/

http://www.rightattitudes.com/2017/03/14/zeigarnik-effect/

https://www.psychologytoday.com/us/blog/tech-support/201404/your-brain-is-nagging-you-here-are-5-ways-make-it-stop

https://www.mirror.co.uk/news/uk-news/worst-mothers-day-gifts-ever-7501146

https://www.faithgateway.com/praying-example-susanna-wesley/#.XNLmpS-ZPPA

https://www.preachingtoday.com/illustrations/2019/may/fighter-jet-forced-to-land-after-self-inflicted-bullet-dama.html

https://www.huffpost.com/entry/friends-health-science_n_7042042

https://www.thespruce.com/cohabitation-facts-and-statistics-2302236

https://www.preachingtoday.com/search/?query=success&type=&sourcename=illustrations&start=51

https://www.scribd.com/read/235005681/Margin-Restoring-Emotional-Physical-Financial-and-Time-Reserves-to-Overloaded-Lives#

https://www.theguardian.com/environment/2018/nov/02/yosemite-couple-death-selfie-photography-travel-blog-taft-point

https://www.theladders.com/career-advice/busy-work-success

Joel Southerland is the pastor of *Peavine Baptist Church* in Rock Spring, Georgia. During his tenure, the church has grown almost one hundred percent. He is married to Sherry, his high school sweetheart, and they have two grown daughters and one grandson. He has a Master's Degree in Leadership from *Liberty University*.

Made in USA - Kendallville, IN
1171563_9781947153172
09 29 2020 0902